HANDLING REPRESSED EMOTIONS

Paying Attention to Feelings You Unconsciously Avoid

Robert R. Henry

Table of Contents

The Truth Behind Repressed Emotion

Repressed Emotions Mental Health Effects

Repressed Emotions Physical Health Effect

Communal Effects on Mental Health

Releasing emotional baggage

Voice Out: Speaking up your emotions

All rights reserved. No part of this publication may be reproduced, distributed, or transmitted in any form or by any means, including photocopying, recording, or other electronic or mechanical methods, without the prior written permission of the publisher, except in the case of brief quotations embodied in critical reviews and certain other noncommercial uses permitted by copyright law.

Copyright © Robert R. Henry, 2022.

The Truth Behind Repressed Emotions

Repression is the unconscious hindering of negative feelings, impulses, memories, and thoughts from your conscious consciousness. First outlined by Sigmund Freud, the objective of this defensive mechanism is to try to diminish emotions of guilt and fear.

However, while repression could initially be beneficial in calming these uncomfortable emotions, it might lead to more worry down the road.

Repressed emotions are sentiments you unintentionally ignore. These are distinct from sensations you consciously push away because they overwhelm you. Repressed emotions might lead to health concerns over time.

What Are Repressed Emotions?
Some individuals express their feelings openly. Others tend to hide them. But

concealing your feelings doesn't always imply you're repressed them.
There's a lot of discussion concerning repressed emotions. There are also various definitions.

Repression typically refers to the tendency to avoid painful sensations. You automatically shove uncomfortable sensations, ideas, or memories out of your mind. This lets you forget them. You may do this for fear of destroying your good self-image. These are unprocessed emotions. But they can still affect your behavior. \sRepressed emotions might be a technique to protect your mind from terrible experiences. This can happen to a youngster who is abused by a parent or caregiver. They could repress the memories of abuse and their feelings. They then become unconscious or partly unaware of them. The abuse still impacts them, though. It could produce relationship troubles in maturity.

Some people have a propensity to automatically avoid bad sensations that undermine their self-image in all situations.
Or, you can consider yourself as always in control of how you feel and attempt to avoid interactions where people talk about their issues. These are oppressive inclinations. You could unconsciously do this so you don't have to feel grief or anxiety. Those sensations might make you feel like you're losing control.

You might've learned to repress your feelings if you were raised in a chaotic home. You learn how to communicate and regulate your emotions as a youngster. Dysfunctional families have folks who haven't obtained therapy for problems like fear, wrath, grief, humiliation
They could also have difficulties like abuse, addiction, or mental illness. But no one talks about such difficulties. This leads to toddlers and adults who conceal their emotions and ignore their own needs.

Repressed emotions can also lead to things like denying feelings, ignoring feelings, avoiding communication, avoiding touch, distrust

Suppression vs. Repression
Suppression is commonly mistaken for repression, another form of defensive mechanism. Where repression requires unknowingly limiting undesired ideas or emotions, suppression is fully voluntary. Specifically, suppression is consciously attempting to forget or not think about uncomfortable or undesired ideas.

Repressed emotions are not the same as suppressed feelings. Suppression happens when you consciously push undesirable ideas, feelings, or memories out of your mind. This is because you don't know what to do with them.

Some individuals call repression shutting down. Sometimes this leads to numbing yourself with browsing on your phone, watching TV, or doing any other activity so you don't have to experience your feelings.

This sort of behavior might be transient. You could do this at your employment when you're upset with a coworker but you still have to work together and accomplish a project. You lay away your sentiments because you don't know what to do with them and then deal with them later at home.

History of Repression
To understand how repression works, it is crucial to look at how Sigmund Freud understood the mind. He conceived of the human mind as being much like an iceberg.
The top of the iceberg that you can see above the sea represents the conscious mind. The half of the iceberg that is submerged below the ocean, yet is still visible, is the preconscious. The majority of the iceberg that lies hidden under the waterline signifies the unconscious. We may not be aware of what lurks in the

unconscious, yet its contents can nonetheless affect our behavior in a variety of different ways.

The unconscious mind has a profound effect on personality and might potentially contribute to psychological suffering.

Several processes at work deliberately keep unwanted thoughts hidden.

Repression is the initial protective mechanism and it is the most significant.

Signs of Repressed Emotions

Your whole emotional and mental wellness is intimately tied to your physical health. Repressed anger or other unpleasant emotions may be connected to an increased risk for things like depression, high blood pressure, heart disease, digestive disorders, infections, poor energy, pain

You can also experience troubles in your relationships. You might have trouble: expressing what you need, experiencing disagreement, feeling connected and personal with people

Accepting unpleasant emotions (rather than rejecting or repressing them) might help people adapt better to stress and contribute to overall psychological wellness.

There may also be certain behavioural symptoms that someone is repressing memories, ideas, or feelings. They could have difficulties communicating their ideas or feelings, even becoming defensive when asked about them. They could feel numb or adopt subconscious activities (such as consuming alcohol or immersing themselves in social media) to escape painful sensations.

You might not know that you repress your feelings. If you have problems in your relationships or you're uncomfortable with unpleasant feelings, these can be evidence that you tend to unintentionally avoid them.

How Repression Is Used

Repression is one method the mind may deal with uncomfortable ideas or feelings. And in certain circumstances, that is useful. Distorting reality via denial most typically improves and enhances psychological and social functioning. People who have what is known as a repressive coping style tend to experience less despair and manage better with pain. It is more frequent in elderly adults, suggesting that it is something that develops with time. It is also related to higher well-being. However, repression can also be employed to avoid addressing uncomfortable events and feelings, and this can have serious effects.

Impact of Repression

Selective forgetting is one technique that humans limit awareness of unwelcome ideas or experiences. One way this might occur is through what is referred to as retrieval-induced forgetfulness.

Retrieval-induced forgetting happens when retrieving particular memories causes other relevant information to be lost. So continuously drawing forth some memories can lead other memories to become less accessible. Traumatic or undesired memories, for example, could be erased by frequent retrieval of more favorable ones.

Dreams\sDreams are one way to peek into the unconscious mind. By evaluating the manifest content of dreams (or the actual events that take place in a dream), we can learn more about the latent content of the dream (or the symbolic, unconscious meanings) (or the symbolic, unconscious meanings).
Repressed sentiments may spring out in the worries, anxieties, and wants that we experience in these dreams.

Slips of the Tongue
Slips of the tongue are another example of how repressed thoughts and feelings may

make themselves known. Mistaken slips of the tongue might be highly illuminating, frequently reflecting what we think or feel about something on an unconscious level.

While these sentiments may be repressed, they have a way of sneaking out when we least expect them. Calling your love partner the name of someone you work with can simply be a simple mistake—but it might be an indication that you have repressed sexual impulses for that co-worker.

The Oedipus Complex

Children go through a phase during the genital stage where they first regard their same-sex parent as a competition for the opposite-sex parent's love. In trying to resolve this conflict, they conceal these thoughts of hostility and instead begin to identify with their same-sex parent.

For boys, these sentiments are known as the Oedipal complex, whereas the similar sensations in young girls are dubbed the Electra complex.

Phobias

Phobias can be an example of how a repressed memory could continue to exert an impact on behavior. For example, a little child is hit by an automobile. They eventually acquire a strong phobia of vehicles but have no recall of when or how this fear arose. They have repressed the terrible recollection of the scary event with the automobile, so they are ignorant of exactly where their dread came from.

It's tempting to disguise your feelings, but it won't do you (or anybody else) any favors.

Say your partner shares information at a family event you requested them to keep hidden. You're unhappy and ashamed, but you pretend everything's OK until you get home, where you can chat alone. You don't want to dispute in front of your extended family and make the situation worse.

Occasional emotional repression normally won't cause difficulties as long as you finally deal with them in healthy, constructive ways. It can become an issue, though, if it becomes a trend and inhibits your capacity to speak genuinely.

Why do people hide feelings?
People often learn to conceal emotions for a few fundamental reasons.

To avoid revealing 'weakness': Showing emotion can put you in a vulnerable situation, and it's very reasonable to desire to avoid exposing vulnerabilities to others.
You could worry expressing certain emotions would lead people to condemn you and assume you can't regulate your sentiments. As a consequence, you hide your grief, anxiety, irritation, and other so-called bad emotions. You might also have some fears regarding someone utilizing these sentiments against you, especially if that's occurred to you previously.

To prevent getting hurt: People typically mask feelings to safeguard their relationships. When someone you care about does something distressing, you could opt to mask your dissatisfaction.

Yes, their behaviour disturbed you. But if they react adversely when you tell them how you feel, you might wind up starting an even more unpleasant conflict. So, instead, you prefer to avoid fighting totally.

This drive to escape suffering typically arises from an underlying lack of confidence in yourself and others. If someone has exploited your emotions in the past, you might worry about trusting someone new with your sentiments. You can also lack trust in your abilities to manage disagreement constructively and productively.

Lack of confidence: If you grow up hearing the message that your thoughts and feelings don't matter, you'll likely learn to repress your sentiments from an early age. This commonly happens when parents and caregivers criticize or criticize you for expressing your feelings. This judgement isn't confined to negative emotions, though. Some restricted caretakers chastise children for any outburst, unpleasant or positive. Eventually, you may no longer feel safe expressing your opinions and feelings, so you hide them to prevent further criticism.

Caregivers who cover their feelings might likewise encourage the impression that you should do the same.

Repressed Emotions Mental Health Effects

In psychology, repression of emotion is an element of emotion control. It is a notion that is founded on an individual's understanding of emotions, which includes sources of emotion, feelings of the body and regarding behaviour that are expressed, and their possible ways of modification

Repression of emotion is the instinctive process by which humans exercise control over the feelings they have, adjusting elements including when and how the emotions are experienced and expressed. Effective management of emotion helps the individual to adaptively cope with a broad range of environmental scenarios. However, when it becomes unequal or unbalanced, it gets widely recognized and its negative results may pose harm to mental health. It may therefore become a possible development or maintenance element in mental illness disorders.

It becomes necessary to comprehend the good and negative repercussions of different emotion regulation systems. In this respect, disagreement is continuing in the area over the implications of purposeful attempts to repress emotion, defined here as intentional attempts to down-regulate the internal experience and outward expression of unpleasant impact. Contradictory predictions come from normative and therapeutic works of literature concerning the implications of such repression of emotion.

Repression of emotion is one of the most prominent ways of managing emotion adopted by humans. Clinical traditions made it clear that the psychological health of an individual depends on how effective impulses are managed or regulated; repressing a physical emotional response while emotionally prompted to express will increase the intensity of the emotional experience as a result of the concentration on repressing the emotion, emotions become increasingly severe or intense the longer they are bottled up.

The Connection with Stress
Stress is related to elevated cortisol levels. Concealing and repressing emotions might give rise to stress-related psychological responses. The onset of stress comes as a result of the societal rejection and punishment of overt emotional expression that induces repression which is itself scary and unpleasant. There are certain fields of human endeavour which require the repression of positive or negative emotions such as estate agents who may hide their happiness when a good offer is tabled for house sake of maintaining their professionalism, or primary school teachers repressing their anger or disappointment sake of upsetting their young pupils when teaching them good morals.
Stress brought about by such extended repression of emotion can induce an

increase in heart rate, anxiety, low level of commitment, and other impacts which can be damaging to the productivity of an individual.

Repression and Depression: The Link
Repression of emotion, as a way to manage emotions, is advantageous in some elements of life such as encouraging ambitious pursuits and delivering fulfillment to hedonic demands. In as much as repression of emotion is viewed as a poor impact on emotional experience, it performs other beneficial roles. Repression of emotion is a goal-oriented approach that is directed by people's beliefs and conventions and maybe by abstract notions about the control of emotion. A reciprocal association occurs between parental support and symptoms of depression however there is no sign of depression with peer victimization.

Masking emotions may have some rather major impacts on physical and mental well-being.

Disrupted communication
By masking your feelings, you inhibit clear contact with the people in your life. This lack of communication makes it challenging to handle conflict. When you can't work through difficulties, they'll probably keep happening. You could ultimately grow angry and resentful, and these sentiments could create the confrontation you hoped to avoid. You might also start avoiding people who evoke particular feelings, risking losing connections you cherish.
Emotional repression may become so much of a habit that it begins to happen unintentionally, thus you could also realize you begin to lose touch with your feelings.

Emotion buildup
Pretending you don't have certain sentiments could help you avoid expressing

them publicly, but it doesn't make them go away. Keeping down your emotions might heighten them.

A classic example of this is the fury. Many individuals feel it's better to tamp down anger than express it. But hiding your anger means you don't confront it, so it continues to rise and seethe behind your mask of serenity. Eventually, when you can't keep it in any longer, you could explode up – and not necessarily towards the person who got you upset.

Relationship strain

You might believe you can disguise your feelings rather well, but those who know you can typically identify when something's hurting you. Insisting "I'm fine" and "Nothing's wrong" might confuse and annoy people when the contrary is true. If they realize you aren't speaking the truth, they could feel wounded by your lack of trust and begin losing trust in you. If they do believe you, they can lose faith in their ability to comprehend you or realize they don't know you as well as they believed. Eventually, people might begin to question the strength of the partnership. In either circumstance, the connection you meant to safeguard still ends up being ruined.

Early death
repressing emotions might contribute to the tension you experience. Unaddressed stress tends to stay in the body, which can contribute to diabetes, sleep disorders, high blood pressure, and heart problems.
Any one of these factors can impair long-term health and lifespan, especially without treatment.

How can you build a healthy mental relationship with your emotions?
It might take time and effort to learn to communicate your sentiments honestly. These tactics can help you grow more comfortable with your emotions and fight the impulse to repress them.

Practice mindfulness: Mindfulness refers to your awareness of the present moment and ability to perceive things as they happen.

Emotional awareness is noticing and embracing feelings as they come up, even if you choose not to express them immediately.

You could think, "Wow, I'm extremely irritated right now. I don't want to start a quarrel, though, so I'm going to take a minute before trying to explain why I'm so upset."

Sitting with emotions helps you to completely feel and comprehend them. This better awareness might make it simpler to grasp your part in the problem and explore alternative solutions.

Share your feelings honestly: Your emotions are part of your life experience. Discounting them might eventually invalidate your identity and sense of self, and impede you from accomplishing your goals. There are methods to convey sentiments, even unpleasant ones, without being impolite. It helps to practice emotional communication by first opening up to loved ones and those you trust. Try utilizing "I" statements to bring up sentiments politely.

For example Two of your buddies continually discussing their beach trip in your group chat – something you weren't included in. Instead of nursing injured sentiments discreetly, you may express, "Hey, I feel kind of left out! Why don't we have a beach hangout next time?"

Respectfully expressing your unhappiness might persuade them to reconsider their decision. Pretending you don't mind conveys the impression that you accept the situation as is.

But since you genuinely don't accept it, you walk away feeling disappointed and bitter. These sentiments can eventually impair your work performance, making a future increase even more improbable.

Talk to someone you trust: If you don't have a chance to express your feelings, talking about them afterward might still help, particularly if you can't change the circumstances.

Say you're battling with a co-worker who frequently makes sharp remarks and does minor things that upset you. You've respectfully requested them to stop and made your employer aware of the matter, yet the conduct persists. At work, you maintain cool and try not to show your displeasure. At home, you rant to your sympathetic partner. Knowing you can share your dissatisfaction later helps you get through the day without getting too fired up.

Keeping a diary can also help you practice expressing feelings as they come up. Journaling may not have nearly the same impact as talking to someone who can validate your sadness, but it may still help you manage tough feelings.

Reaching out: When hiding emotions has been a long-standing routine, you could struggle to change this behavior alone.

Talking to a therapist can help you learn to better emotional expression. Your therapist can help you discover probable causes for emotional repression, including trust concerns and fears of rejection, and begin addressing these aspects. Therapy also gives a safe area to focus on being more in touch with your feelings.

Once you feel more comfortable with your emotions, a therapist can: teach you good communication and conflict resolution skills give suggestions on techniques to cope with overwhelming sensations to help you treat mental health issues, such as worry and stress, connected with buried emotions

In summary, occasionally hiding emotions is very typical. It could even appear like the greatest option in uncomfortable or public settings.

But when you repress your feelings because you worry about how others will respond, you end up rejecting your own experience. This could seem like a smart approach to avoid confrontation and emotional anguish, but it generally comes back to bite your mental well-being in the end.

Learning to express emotions genuinely isn't always simple, but simply following the guidelines in this book will enable you to speak more openly, without allowing fear of the potential repercussions holds you back.

Repressed Emotions Physical Health Effects

How many times have you heard this advice on dealing with difficult emotions? "Stop being so touchy. Suck it up and go on."

When people encourage you to bury your feelings, it makes you question yourself and the messages your body is attempting to give to you. Think about how many times today you've sought to push away an unpleasant sensation by browsing through social media, bingeing on Netflix, or using food, drink, or addictive substances to escape feelings. In a society packed with diversions and with the invalidating messages we've gotten throughout our lives about emotions, it's simple to see why so many people are terrified of feeling.

We've been trained to ignore, reject, and avoid our emotions—but this is more than simply terrible advice. Feeling leads to healing. When we push away, repress, or condemn ourselves for experiencing emotions, it comes with a very high cost: our health.

Avoiding emotions might hijack your health. We've learned how to push it aside, yet even when we do, it always stays—and increases. When we hide our emotions, we're making them stronger. This can generate various illnesses in the body and the mind, creating a plethora of health difficulties.

When you conceal your emotions, you are confusing and harming your body in a significant way. Emotions are our body's method of getting us to take action. On a very primitive level, our bodies are attempting to keep us safe at all times. Back in the caveman and cavewoman days, we learned to listen to our guts because they would rescue us from attack: run away or get devoured. People today are not necessarily running from wild creatures anymore but responding to emotion and processing it can still eventually protect them from risks, both physical and mental.

With the rush of our days, it might be tough to hear what our bodies are trying to communicate, yet when we disregard those warnings, we can still suffer immensely.

repressing emotions is related to high rates of heart disease, as well as autoimmune illnesses, ulcers, IBS, and gastrointestinal health issues. Whether you are experiencing rage, sadness, loss, or irritation, putting those feelings aside leads to physical stress on your body. Holding in feelings has a tie to high cortisol—the hormone generated in reaction to stress—and that cortisol leads to decreased immunity and damaging thought habits. Over time, untreated or unacknowledged stress can lead to an increased risk of diabetes, issues with memory, aggressiveness, anxiety, and depression.

In other words, opting to bury your sentiments, ignore them, internalize them, pretend they didn't happen or tell yourself that there is no need to deal with them can physically make you sick from the stress.

People who consistently fail to deal with their emotions honestly and fully are likewise prone to have greater interpersonal issues. They are less conscious of the messages they are giving to others and are typically more reactive and distant from themselves, which can lead to feelings of isolation and can interfere with relationships.

We assume a person who conceals their feelings would be a fully distant, possibly chilly, and low-energy person; this is by no means true in all instances. On the contrary, ignoring a thorough grasp of our emotions and what's driving them might lead us to get locked in a fight-or-flight response. Something provokes an emotional reaction, and suddenly we could start to obsess over all the things that are unpleasant and convince ourselves that the most horrible outcomes that might happen absolutely will happen. It's just fear. This increases your body's stress reaction and drives you into a state of high arousal. That's when the cortisol surges, a chemical called norepinephrine is released that ups your heart rate and blood pressure, and you might get so keyed up on fear that you don't take the time to properly grasp the event that drove you into this response. You don't take the time to examine if you perceived the stressor appropriately.

How can you build a healthy physical relationship with your emotions?
Listening to our emotions is daunting and might feel incredibly odd. You've spent most of your life avoiding them, so why on earth would you want to feel them all at once? That's unhealthy too. It can cause too much confusion. Instead, educate yourself on the science of emotions (which you already have done if you read the above) and practice a couple of the techniques below. The objective is to move slowly—this helps you

acquire confidence in what you're feeling and learn to trust your emotions rather than ignore them.

Step 1: Breath.
Take time to become aware of how your body is feeling during the day. Try to set an alarm or reminder for the morning and midafternoon merely to remind yourself to check in and take a few deep breaths. No matter what you are doing, take a few seconds. Are you tense? If so, where? Are you breathing in a deep way or in a shallow way? How does it feel to take a few deep breaths? By doing this, you can begin to discover where sensations are lodged in your body. Then via diaphragmatic breathing (deep breathing as your stomach pushes out on the inhale), you can stimulate your vagus nerve. This nerve is crucial for regulating emotions, and when we take deep thoughtful breaths, we are massaging the strength of our feelings.

Step 2: Identify one feeling at a time.
Simply admitting your feeling decreases the intensity of emotions, making them tremendously simpler to manage. Your amygdala, the emotional center of the brain, becomes trapped in an unreasonable thought process when you seek to repress your feelings. When you attempt to escape what you are feeling, you aren't fixing anything, and your brain will get stuck. When you recognize what is upsetting you—"I'm feeling stressed right now"—your frontal brain gets to work. That brain area assists with problem-solving discovering answers and validates your experience, which might help you start to feel better.

Step 3: Be gentle to your mind.
We as humans all have emotions. Some of them are positive; other ones, are not so much. Practice self-compassion; try not to invalidate yourself with dismissive or harmful self-talk about what you are feeling. If you're unhappy with the way someone

talked to you, it's appropriate to feel annoyance or grief; it's not an opportunity to transform this into an unjustified critique of yourself. This merely causes your cortisol levels to soar, resulting in more stress and more worry, and more negative thoughts.

When we stop and recognize our feelings, this helps to rephrase our thinking more kindly and compassionately, such as how you would say to a kid or close friend. When we are kind to ourselves, it can stop the surge of cortisol and help us regulate healthily. Self-compassion may be a significant trigger for the production of oxytocin, a soothing and relaxing hormone that helps us feel connected in a good manner and may take a dramatic scenario down a few notches quickly.

Step 4: Practice mindfulness.

When we learn to tune into our bodies, our thoughts slow down and provide us more control. Our brains are extremely amazing—studies suggest that meditation practice reduces reactivity to stress and may modify our reactions to emotions, benefiting our emotional and physical health. Short, guided meditations (two to five minutes) are a fantastic technique to move one's mind off of autopilot and lessen avoidance of emotion. Doing this regularly (preferably in the morning but whatever works for you) can help you become more self-aware.

Being conscious of and understanding your emotions enhances your mental and physical health without a doubt. This is the actual definition of self-care and may help everyone enhance their well-being. If you assume that concealing or burying your sentiments won't generate adverse impacts on your mind and body, you are incorrect. While it might be terrifying and painful to face your negative feelings, it will allow you to discover a place of understanding and enhance your general quality of everyday life.

Communal Effects on Mental Health

Relationships are one of the most crucial components of our existence. Persons who are more socially attached to family, friends, or their community are happier, physically healthier and live longer, with fewer mental health issues than people who are less well connected.

It's not simply the number of friends you have, and it's not whether or not you're in a committed relationship, but it's the quality of your connections that matters. Living in conflict or within a toxic relationship is more damaging than being alone.

Family and childhood
Childhood conditions such as inadequate attachment, neglect, abuse, lack of quality stimulation, conflict, and family disintegration can negatively influence future social conduct, educational outcomes, career position, and mental and physical health.

Conversely, children and young adults who have solid personal and social interactions with family and friends have greater levels of well-being. Family relationship difficulties are the single largest presenting difficulty. Preventative treatments with parents that focus on their connection as a pair can assist to boost children's welfare and decrease emotional and behavioral challenges.

Couple relationships
Being happily married or in a secure relationship benefits favorably mental health. High marital quality is related to decreased stress and less depression. However, single persons have better mental health results than people who are unhappily married. Negative social interactions and relationships, especially with partners/spouses, raise the risk of depression, anxiety, and suicidal thoughts, whereas good interactions lessen the risk of these difficulties.

Community

People in communities with higher levels of social cohesiveness report lower rates of mental health problems than those in neighborhoods with lower cohesion, regardless of how disadvantaged or rich a community is. Neighbourhood social cohesiveness is connected with a decrease in depression symptoms in older adults.

The community can be described in physical and emotional ways.

Physically, a community might be a shared area or a collection of individuals that share some common denominator.

Emotionally, the community is characterized as a sense of camaraderie or similarity with others. The community also denotes the relationship one has with their environment, including the people and places that make it.

Ultimately, there is an overriding concept of oneness that transcends the multiple senses of the term.

How to Find Your Community

We have all experienced community in one way or another. Maybe you played sports in high school and resided in the Northeast section of your city. There are various techniques you may use when developing a community or cultivating your feeling of community. You can:

Explore your interests. Becoming engaged with these sorts of activities can introduce you to individuals who appreciate what you enjoy, making it even simpler to connect with them. Some examples of these activities may be joining a leisure sports team or enrolling in pottery courses or reading club.

Follow your values. How do you believe the world might be better? What role can you play in making those improvements?

Determining your beliefs and finding activities that coincide with them is a terrific way for you to discover a community and give back to it. This might involve working for a charity or nonprofit group.

Strengthen your convictions. People typically hold onto their views with considerable conviction. Seeking activities and groups of people that display similar ideas might push you to take additional action in pursuit of a shared goal or inspire you to pursue personal objectives as well. Some examples of belief-based activities may be joining a church or political group. You desire to engage in, or with, activities and people that mean something to you. It just makes sense that you would enjoy and interact more with things you are enthusiastic about. By discovering activities and people that fit with what is significant to you, you will likely find that a feeling of community comes naturally.

The overriding notion of togetherness that distinguishes a community is precisely what makes it so powerful on individuals' mental health. The links, connections, and interactions facilitated by togetherness are how people of a community can benefit from one another and from the group as a whole. Significant research has been done to show one fundamental point: Humans are social organisms. We are not designed to be alone in this world, and learning from one another is how the world continues to progress.

The value of meaningful relationships, connections, and interactions on a person's mental well-being cannot be underestimated. Children and adolescents are substantially more likely to have greater levels of well-being if they have solid personal and social ties. In the study of couple psychology, being in a good marriage or stable relationship is connected with decreased stress and depression rates.

Concerning the community as a whole, communities with greater levels of social cohesiveness suffer lower rates of mental health problems than areas with lower social cohesion, independent of how affluent or poor the neighborhood is.

As social creatures, we all require community. For those who already have it, it's a key aspect of preserving mental health. For those who don't, searching out community- whether it's through an online community, neighbors, old friends, work colleagues, or even engaging a therapist, may substantially enhance someone's quality of life.

Belonging: Just like food and water, the sense of acceptance and identity with a group is believed to be a human necessity. A sense of belonging, for most individuals, is vital to the value they place on life. More than merely being a member of a group, a sense of belonging is satisfied when you can put your most honest self on the show and be met with favorable responses that suggest you are among others who love your nature. Belonging to a community may enhance your mental health because it provides a space that encourages you to be yourself and one that links you with individuals who are similar to you.

Security: Similar to belonging, a sense of security is regarded as one of the most fundamental human needs. A sense of security refers to a feeling of confidence and safety. The most important part of a sense of security is that the confidence and safety felt are not reserved for just one location or community. A sense of security can help people feel more secure while confronting new events and engaging with new people. A community provides you the chance to trust and depend on people, and the more comfortable you feel doing so, the more likely you are to exhibit that in other circumstances.

Support: Several studies have demonstrated that having a support system has significant benefits on a person's overall well-being. Strong support systems have been demonstrated to alleviate anxiety and depression and increase coping skills. People with robust support systems have also exhibited better immune systems and decreased risks of early mortality. Communities give a cohort of persons to rely on for support and who presumably care about you and wish to be an outlet for you. Knowing you have people who care about you to support you through difficult times may make surviving much easier since you won't ever feel utterly alone.

Purpose: Especially when forming a community through channels based on values and ideas, such as political groups or churches, being a member of a community may make you feel a part of something greater than yourself. By extending the importance you place on your life to the way you influence your surroundings, belonging to a community may help you build a deeper sense of purpose. Having a feeling of purpose may affect your behavior, define new objectives, and give you a sense of direction in your life. It typically promotes mental health since it may drive you to deal with difficult situations more productively or it may reduce some of your situational strain since, whichever it works out, you keep the reassuring presence of your mission.

While all the aforementioned benefits of community in increasing mental well-being are genuine, they may not be adequate for keeping your mental health difficulties under control. With the combined effects of the benefits listed above, another profound effect of community on mental health is that it often makes seeking mental health care easier and more approachable. A sense of belonging to a group can offer the certainty that you will not be outcasted or made to feel incapable of seeking professional care. A sense of security can give you the confidence needed to try new experiences, like talking to a therapist, and the trust you've developed in people through your community may allow you to open up more in therapy. Having a support system of people who care about you and your well-being may give reminders about the significance of your health and can provide the encouragement needed to continue with mental health treatment even if it gets challenging. Finally, a feeling of purpose might encourage you to conceive of your health and general well-being as deeper than simply yourself since you play a vital part in the lives of others.

In the same way that mental health greatly impacts our quality of life, the kind of people we spend our lives with heavily influences our mental health. Being an involved part of a community, or several, helps us give significance to our everyday acts and experiences. It is encouraging to be linked to more than just oneself, and for some, the motivation obtained from being accountable to others may motivate us to be better. The combined presence of a sense of belonging, security, support, and purpose is ultimately the outcome of being around people who care about you.

Communities are filled with individuals who care about one another, and who thus, empower each other to care for themselves as well. Finding the appropriate community for you might not happen on the first try, but press on, because they are out there. Whether you have a community and are looking to expand, realized who you thought was your community is not healthy for you, or are just beginning to search for your people, know that there are so many others in the same predicament as you, so there is no need to feel alone at any stage of the process. Finally, bear in mind that much as finding a community will enhance your life, the members of your prospective community will greatly benefit from your participation in their lives.

Releasing emotional baggage

You've probably heard the term "emotional baggage." It's frequently used to explain the phenomena of carrying prior trauma or so-called bad events into life, relationships, or a job. You may notice this mirrored in someone's posture as if they're lugging about an awful weight. It may even prohibit them from moving on in life.
Everyone carries unresolved emotions from events to some degree. However, feelings that aren't dealt with don't just go away.

They can affect the way you think about yourself, how you react to stress, your physical well-being, and your relationships with others.
After all, emotional baggage gets its name from someplace, right? Let's uncover the layers of how and where emotions become lodged, so you may release what's pulling you down.

What does it mean to have 'trapped' emotions?

Perhaps you've heard of individuals sobbing during yoga, massage, or acupuncture therapy because of a delicate place that, when triggered, appears to lead to an emotional release. Though some may speak to trauma as "stored" or "trapped" in the body, it isn't always a scientific way to state it. However, the effects of severe stress can emerge physically.

This may be because the brain identifies this location with a particular memory – frequently on a subconscious level.

Activating particular regions of the body may elicit these memories. Emotions are continually being formed – unconsciously or consciously — in reaction to the retrieval of memories or frustrated aspirations. Touch may bring up emotions or memory may trigger feelings in a particular location of the body. While this is normally connected with a corporeal location, everything is happening in the brain. Alternatively, trauma and tough emotions can become genuinely trapped energy in the body. Trapped emotional vibrations induce neighboring tissues to resonate at the same frequency, known as resonance. Each repressed emotion lives in a unique spot in the body, pulsating at its distinct frequency. This may cause you to attract more of that feeling, causing a build-up or blockage.

How can emotions get trapped?
The mind-body link, or the concept that a person's mental and emotional wellness affects the status of their physical health.
A typical example of this is fear.
If you're in a circumstance where you're terrified, your body develops a physical response to this feeling by triggering the fight-flight-freeze response.
Three things happen when an emotion is experienced.
We build an emotional vibe.

We feel the emotion and any thoughts or bodily sensations related to it.
This is where the mind and body's interconnectivity comes into play.
We move on from the feeling by digesting it. Emotional processing happens in the limbic regions of the brain. We're continually taking in information, which creates pre-conscious autonomic nervous system responses. This sends a signal to the body generating the associated emotion.

In other words, your "feeling" stems from what your neurological system is telling you. When the second or third process indicated above gets stopped, the energy of the emotion becomes stuck in the body. As a result, you can have muscle tension, soreness, or other problems. The more emotional intensity, the more probable it is to become imprisoned.

The expression 'trapped emotions' typically signifies that the genuine self wants to say something that the fake self doesn't want us to express. In psychology, we think of the real self as the part of ourselves that we are born with that is naturally open, inquiring, and trusting, while the false self arises as a collection of adaptive methods to deal with sorrow and loss. This repressed negative emotional energy might emerge as hostility, poor decision-making, self-sabotage, overreaction, increased stress, and anxiety depression and fatigue

Trapped emotions can be compared to dragging around a huge burden. It weighs us down, impairs our attitude, and drains our vitality. Additionally, it can potentially harm biological tissues and hinder the regular activities of organs and glands.

Trapped emotions and trauma
It's hard to have a discourse about imprisoned emotions without examining trauma, especially how the brain processes

it. Nearly everyone suffers trauma at some time in their lives.

Trauma may come about from life situations like a divorce, a big life change, the death of a loved one, adultery in a relationship, loss of a job, an experience of violence, discrimination, or racism

Trauma can influence cognitive functions. It notably impacts memory processing and the capacity to recall factual information or explicit memory. As a result, the painful event or memory is not "logged" properly in the brain. When it comes to an overpowering encounter, such as a trauma, the brain stores the unpleasant memories as visuals or physical sensations.

When triggered, the brain may disengage from reality or recreate the traumatic event in the form of a flashback. This is known as dissociation or psychological separation.

These sensory pieces persist in the mind and impede the brain's normal recuperation process. Traumatic memories are like a virus in our encoding system, where unprocessed experiences may cause our mental and bodily systems to fail.

When trauma isn't processed or healed on its own, it may remain well past the original occurrence. This is typically found in persons with post-traumatic stress disorder (PTSD), a condition that develops when a person endures horrific or life-threatening situations. Those with present PTSD have a smaller hippocampus, a hub for emotions and memories in the brain.

Stress leads to the release of the hormone cortisol, which is a component of the fight-flight-freeze response. Prolonged stress affects the hippocampus, which may show up as irregular blood flow or diminished size. As a result, your body may stay in this hypervigilant state even if you're not consciously thinking of the traumatic incident.

Where are imprisoned emotions kept in the body?

Ever experience a tightening in your chest during an anxiety-inducing situation? Or do you realize that it feels pleasant to extend your hips after an emotionally exhausting day? Where one individual experiences tightness or sensitivity in their body could not be the same for another.

Diverse emotions are connected with different body experiences that are typically the same for individuals.

For example, wrath, fear, and anxiety revealed greater activity in the chest and upper torso. This may explain the origins of idioms like "hot-headed" or "carrying the weight of the world on your shoulders."

These emotions can also stimulate the sympathetic nervous system to cause a fast response in the body. That's why you may feel your heart pumping or your muscles tightening when you become tense.

Feelings are divided into five groups:
Negative, such as stress, wrath, and humiliation
Positive, such as happiness, love, and pride
Cognition, such as attention and perception
Homeostatic states, or a balanced, controlled internal state
Illnesses and somatic states

Unprocessed emotions
Emotions that aren't handled may get retained in your unconscious, and may even impact your physical posture. Your head is in a different posture when you're confident and when you're puzzled, your spine takes on a different form whether you're defeated or successful. People may automatically revert to particular postures that inhibit their awareness of uncomfortable experiences. Muscle tension occurs to establish and sustain postures that keep oneself secure or unconscious of unpleasant sensations. Certain postures and gestures also correspond to distinct sentiments and

social connotations. Think of a loving embrace vs folded arms.
This may help us understand why some feel stress in the body is related to certain regions.

How to discharge emotions from the body
Ever felt like you need to weep, scream, laugh, pound a pillow, or dance it out? We're typically encouraged to hide our pain and soldier on. Over time, this might lead to repressed emotions, often known as unconscious avoidance.

Here are a few strategies to release repressed emotions: admitting your feelings, going through trauma, doing shadow work, creating mindful movement, practicing stillness, and addressing your feelings. The better you understand your emotional environment, the more you can digest your feelings in healthy ways.
The first stage is to connect with and understand your emotions. People with

repressed emotions may have problems identifying their feelings, which is why it might be useful to discuss with a mental health expert. Labeling your feelings might diminish their intensity.
You can accomplish this by employing psychological tools, such as the cognitive distortion categories, or by researching methods to organize your emotions to help you make sense of them.

Work through old trauma
Often, there are things we carry around for years that stretch back to childhood. Some examples of prior trauma include abuse, including mental, emotional, physical, or sexual neglect, loss of a loved one, separation from a parent or caregiver\sbullying and dysfunction at home. Unresolved childhood trauma can show up in numerous ways, including self-blaming, throwing blame on others, feeling melancholy, and withdrawing from social activities

To get past trauma, it's necessary to feel the pain about the reality that you may never obtain what you desired or deserved years ago. Once you've given yourself that sadness, you may acknowledge the adaptive approach you formed as a result.

For example, you may have created a coping method to be independent that finally ends in feelings of loneliness. Without identifying your technique, you can assume you're being alienated by others. On the other hand, if you know that isolation arises from your adaptive approach, you may pinpoint the basis of the issue and alter your strategy to better suit your underlying requirements.

Shadow work

Similar to studying childhood trauma, shadow work gives another perspective of analyzing different elements of ourselves that we keep concealed, generally due to shame or inadequacy. People prefer to hide the aspects of themselves that they consider undesirable.

For example, were you advised to "keep shut" or "stop crying" when you were sad as a kid? This emotional invalidation may drive you to feel embarrassed about your feelings or to downplay them.

Shadow work may be done in numerous ways, however, it's normally encouraged to work with a therapist. You can find a few shadow work activities below:

Intentional movement

Somatic experience (SE) is a means to treat any unresolved tension or emotion that may be remaining in your body. SE uses a body-first approach to address symptoms, with the idea that freeing unprocessed trauma can promote emotional healing. One way to do this is through intentional movement, when we intentionally move, we can create a sense of safety in our bodies that we may not have experienced before, especially for individuals who have stored trauma.

Examples of intentional movement include dance, stretching, yoga, shaking, martial arts, meditative walking, and belly breathing exercises.

Intentional movement releases any stored energy while helping the brain perceive the difference between tension and relaxation.

Practicing stillness

Being motionless allows us to be with our thoughts and feelings in a present condition. It taps into the brain's default mode network, which is when your brain momentarily enters an idle state. This generates what psychologists term "self-generated cognition," which includes things like daydreaming or letting your thoughts wander.

By briefly disengaging from outward stimuli, we may better connect with our inner thoughts, feelings, and desires. We live in a culture where silence isn't practiced enough, nor is it respected, but can be so nourishing to our brains and bodies, it also offers room for emotions to emerge into... awareness.

Some strategies to cultivate stillness are: meditation, breathing exercises, sitting in nature, listening to relaxing music, repeating affirmations, and progressive muscle relaxation

The bottom line: When an emotion is not properly processed, it may become "stuck" in the body. However, it's the limbic regions of the brain where emotional processing happens. While certain portions of your body surely store tension or may be related to an emotional event, ultimately it's the brain that's recreating the emotion. By employing ways to work with your emotions, such as counseling, mindful movement, and shadow work, you may learn to move on from previous traumas and relieve the corresponding body tension.

Voice Out: Speaking up your emotions

Despite a lot of encouragement, political liberties, and psychiatric exhortations, we suffer, nonetheless, most of us, in quiet. We don't exactly express – until it is much too late – what is wrong, what we desire, how we are upset, what we're embarrassed by, and the way we would like things to be.

It shouldn't possibly really be a surprise how hard the speaking out continues to feel. For most of the history of humanity, speaking up was about the most perilous thing an average human could do. There were great authorities above us, who required perfect obedience and were strictly disinterested in whatever we might have to say. Speaking up would have got one flogged, excommunicated, or murdered. Democracy is, at most, some two hundred and fifty years old and our psychological progress has a propensity of lagging well beyond our social reality. Long after a battle is finished, we respond with the worries of the hunted, and centuries after the last feudal lord moved into an apartment in town, we behave with some of the meek humility of the cowed serf. In personal life, the same ideas of subordination have applied. Throughout history, a decent child did not speak up in any form. If we were sad, we sobbed gently under our pillow at night. If we unintentionally spilled any ink, we'd try to disguise the evidence. The adult does not have to be an obvious bully to cripple a youngster. If they are often on edge (preoccupied with things at work), look despondent and near to collapse, or have exalted yet inflexible expectations of who their kid should be, the youngster might as well wear a belt around their lips.

So most of the year's human beings have been on this earth, it's been a narrative of festering, sulking, bitterness, restrained wrath, bitten lips – and of speaking, publicly, nothing.

Only very recently, in the last second from an evolutionary standpoint, have we awoken to the probable advantages and sometimes need of speaking up.

We know that it is excellent in offices if those lower down the company speak out to those at the top. We know that it is good, in love, if partners who feel offended and unhappy about anything (however minor and trivial it might appear) speak out, to be able to feel affection and desire once again. We know in families that it is helpful if youngsters manage to tell their parents they're not interested in certain types of occupations or complain if they are being mistreated.

But the legacies of our unfreedom abound. We smile a bit too freely, we strive a little too hard to soothe; we are a little too sluggish to voice a hurt. We aren't, in this regard, pleasant; we're terrified and humiliated. Our friendship is formed not out of choice, but out of an unwillingness to dare to cause upset.

To learn to speak up involves two fairly odd-sounding things.

Firstly, a knowledge that, at some level, we are terrified, afraid that if we speak we will be murdered. It seems bizarre and embarrassing, but it is how tiny children feel after dad has slammed the door or mom has shouted enough times 'you'll be the end of me', and it is in the early imagination that our vision of what will happen if we speak is first established.

Secondly, we need to realize, in our mature moments, the grownup fact that we will not after all be killed, since enough people have already died on our behalf to give us the freedom of expression and our ability to cross town and start a new life someplace else. We need to transfer what is codified in law into what eventually seems real to us psychologically – and, fearlessly, speak up.

Speaking up isn't always easy. Depending on who is around, where you are and what the current topic of conversation is, it might be hard to find the bravery to speak your opinion. Here are three reasons why you should be standing out for yourself more regularly.

It might make you more confident: Nobody else knows what it's like to be your unique self. You had your own, independent views and opinions and they deserved to be shared. Don't be ashamed or scared of your thoughts, be proud of them. Over time, this will grow easier and you'll find yourself hesitating less and speaking out more whether it's at the job or in your personal life.

It can motivate others to speak up: Your ideas can enlighten individuals and help them build their own opinions. Maybe you can offer them a new perspective that they've never considered before. They could agree and speak up with you but even if they don't, that's all right. It just takes one person to start a chain reaction.

It benefits your entire mental health: Keeping things bottled up within might generate tension and harm your general mental health. It might affect other elements of your life. The dissatisfaction you are attempting to hold away might intrude into your career, relationships, fitness, and more. So when in doubt, let it out!

Speaking up is scary, there is no doubt about it. It is also one of the most empowering gestures you can perform for yourself. It doesn't require anyone or anything else, just you and your voice. Remember, you can speak, when others may not. Don't allow the gift of your voice to go to waste. You can be the voice that others don't have.

Why Is Bottling Up Your Emotions Bad for You?

Bottling up your emotions involves repressing your innermost sentiments. It is when you resist venting out what you feel. There is the concern that you may look weak or just prefer keeping your feelings to yourself, which is typical. It's like sweeping the dirt under the rug and maintaining the lid of a boiling pot.

The reality is, you can't ignore these emotions, and they don't go away that simply. Bottling up your feelings is never helpful for the mind and body. Your physical and mental health is dramatically damaged when you repress your feelings. Bottling up negative emotions like worry and anger can impede the regular operation of your stress chemicals called cortisol. This leads to reduced immune function and an increased chance of getting a chronic disease. Not expressing your feelings is also a pathway to acquiring mental health disorders.

What Happens When You Bottle Up Your Feelings?

Everyone must learn how to express their emotions healthily. The first stage is awareness or knowing the signals if you're bottling up your feelings and realizing the ramifications if this continues.

What happens when you bottle up your feelings?

1. You feel concerned and nervous all the time: If you choose not to deal with your feelings, these bottled-up emotions start to come out of nowhere, making you feel worried and anxious all the time. Let's imagine you're suffering financial troubles and don't communicate this with your spouse. No matter how you maintain this hidden, the sentiments creep up and you feel frightened and nervous all the time. But when you talk up your money troubles to your partner, you will feel better. You will receive the assistance you need, and your spouse may help you with the budgeting.

2. You resort to unhealthy coping mechanisms: Some people tend to resort to unhealthy coping mechanisms when they have too many emotions to mask. Other people drink all night to forget their problems. And then some resort to substance abuse to have that euphoric feeling and avoid getting frustrated. Others express their negative emotions in an unhealthy way by lashing out at their loved ones.

Some harm themselves or have suicidal thoughts because their emotions are too much to handle. These unhealthy coping mechanisms will not do you any good. They are all self-destructive behaviors that will harm you and hurt those who care about you. You can avoid all of these if you let all your thoughts and emotions out in a healthy way.

3. There are changes in your eating patterns: Have you heard of the saying "eating your feelings away"? Have you seen someone not eat at all because they're suffering too much pain? Yes, bottling up your emotions may badly affect your eating behaviors. As a result, you either gain or lose weight. Many individuals can relate to this. What people don't recognize immediately away is that changes in the way they eat have effects on their physical health and emotional well-being.

4. You get frequent headaches: Are you having a hard time regulating your emotions that it's causing you to have regular headaches? There are instances when you think you're having a physical condition. But the reality is, you're bottling up too many feelings. Perhaps you're spending too much time thinking about negative ideas that it's giving you recurring headaches. When this happens, you may have a hard time concentrating at work, find yourself easily

distracted, and feel grumpy all day. It's no surprise how bottling up your emotional pain can affect your everyday life by manifesting as physical pain.

5. You find it hard to communicate your feelings: If you're used to bottling up your emotions for a long time, you may find it hard to articulate what you genuinely feel. This is not healthy for your mental health. Do you aware that bottling up your emotions may lead to depression and anxiety disorders? If you always choose to keep your sentiments to yourself, you won't know when to confront them. Expressing emotions may feel unusual to you that you don't consider it an option anymore, which may be rather typical among guys. Expressing what you feel is a tremendous sort of relief. Keeping your concerns to yourself can only lead to overthinking and feeling nervous for lengthy durations.

6. You overreact to everything: Because of all the repressed emotions, you find it hard to deal with stress and start overreacting to everything. For instance, you're having a meeting at work, and what's intended to be a brainstorming session feels like a personal assault on you because you're overreacting. Sometimes, this reaction is a cry for aid. You need to vent out; instead, you lash out at the people around you. A simple chat causes you to break down into tears and have aggressive outbursts. Not only are you coping with your anger the incorrect way, but you're also destroying your relationships.

7. You avoid confrontation: Because you don't want to deal with your feelings, you strive to avoid conflict. You have a hard time addressing your worries, making it tough for you to get the point over. Being involved in a confrontation makes you anxious and nervous. The fact is, avoiding fights doesn't make the issue go away.

How to Stop Bottling Up Your Emotions

Before you suffer another breakdown, understand how to quit bottling up your feelings. You may find it tough at first but consider this as creating a connection to your inner self and taking care of your mental health.

Learn how to quit bottling up your emotions with these techniques.

1. Know the reason for your bad emotions: Determining the origin of an unresolved feeling takes time and patience. In time, you'll learn how to recognize your challenges. Once you do, it's going to be simpler for you to deal with your anger, tension, and negative emotions. How can you figure out what generates your unpleasant emotions? Self-reflect and ask yourself these questions:

What am I feeling? Am I angry, terrified, jealous, or anxious?

When did this feeling start? Did I encounter a life event that triggered this? Is it due to heartbreak? Losing a job?

Do these sentiments take up most of my day? Is it time to make some changes?

How are my relationships with my family and loved ones? How's the mood at home? Do my emotions affect my relationship with my loved ones? Where are all these sensations coming from?

2. Record a journal to take care of your mental health: You can make it simpler to reflect on your ideas and feelings if you write them in a journal. Studies demonstrate that journaling may lower stress, help you healthily address problems, and enhance your mental health. Write down what you feel during the day, why you believe you felt that way, or what drove you to respond to anything. You don't need to write every day. Perhaps you can open your journal and let the emotions out when the feelings are too strong. Journaling has

several benefits; it may help you recognize your worries, prioritize problems, and monitor triggering indicators of bottled-up emotions. Writing in a diary and reviewing it in the future is like talking to oneself, so you learn to understand yourself more.

3. Take care of your physical health: Bottled-up emotions can be addressed healthily through exercise and other physical activities.

All the terrible feelings might make you feel overwhelmed. But when you take care of your physical health via exercise, you release pent-up emotions healthily. In addition, after exercise, your body produces happy hormones called endorphins. This makes you feel better, helps you avoid depression and anxiety, and attain a positive body image. When you start to take care of your body, taking care of your mental health follows as well.

4. Talk to someone: The greatest technique to vent out bottled-up feelings is to talk to someone. Are you having marriage problems? Talk to your partner. Are you having issues at work? Have a professional chat with a coworker, or just contact your buddy and talk about what you feel. Sometimes all you need is someone to talk to. Are you experiencing trouble with your kids? Maybe you can chat with your parents or in-laws to obtain their opinion on what you need to do.

Simply talk to someone you trust who will listen to you without judgment. If you find it hard opening up to a person you know, you may always go to a counselor or therapist.

5. Talk to a therapist or counselor: Bottled-up emotions are hard to process. For some, it may be a stroll in the park, while for others, it is tough to unleash their feelings. If you don't comprehend your inner thoughts or know how to deal with your

bottled-up emotions, a therapist can help you analyze what you're going through.

Printed in Great Britain
by Amazon